The Black Woman's Escape Plan to Build a
Purpose-Driven and Profitable Business

F!
THE
GLASS
CEILING

DR. CHERITA WEATHERSPOON

F! The Glass Ceiling: The Black Woman's Escape Plan to Build a Purpose-Driven and Profitable Business

©2025. Cherita Weatherspoon

ISBN: 978-1-952870-10-1 (ebook)
ISBN: 978-1-952870-09-5 (paperback)

Interior Book Design: Amit Dey (amitdey2528@gmail.com)

Published by Spoonfed Motivation Publications

To order additional copies of this book, visit, cheritaweatherspoon. com. For bulk orders, submit your inquiry at cheritaweatherspoon. com/support.

Disclaimer:

Dedication

To the powerhouse women
who make it happen for everyone else…
it's time to make it happen for you.

Contents

PART 1:

The Foundation

1

Forget the Glass Ceiling and Own Your Value as a Leader and CEO

Recognizing Your Worth

You've climbed, you've led, and you've achieved. You've mastered every role, built a reputation of excellence, and earned the respect of peers and superiors alike. But now, as you consider moving from traditional employment in corporate, non-profit, or education to entrepreneurship, you may be questioning, "Can I be as successful in my own business as I am in my career?"

The answer is a resounding "YES!" The skills, knowledge, and experience that led to your success in your career are exactly what will make you a powerhouse as an entrepreneur. Yet, you may still find yourself facing one of the biggest challenges many high-achieving Black women face as they consider transitioning into entrepreneurship; internalizing the value they bring to the table. This book will help you shift that mindset.

In this chapter, you'll learn to see yourself as the powerful and valuable asset you are. You'll redefine your professional accomplishments as marketable value and embrace the confidence and "boss" mentality necessary to step into your role as a CEO.

Free Yourself from Employee Thinking

Reframing Your Experience as Assets

You've built a career, and with it, an arsenal of skills and experience that others need. But often, we don't think of our day-to-day responsibilities as marketable assets. So, let's start by redefining what you already know: your expertise.

Ask yourself these questions:

- What knowledge have I gained that sets me apart?
- What skills have I developed that others find valuable?
- How do I solve problems in ways that others can't?

Each of your responses points to something significant. As an entrepreneur, you can leverage the things that come naturally to you as the foundation for a business. Imagine that all your years of navigating complex projects, leading people, and solving problems have been preparing you for this moment and equipping you with a skill set that makes you valuable in the marketplace… beyond your status as an employee.

Expanding on Your Expertise

Now, let's take this a step further. Think about your career highlights. These might include leading a successful project, mentoring a new employee, or innovating a solution that solved a critical problem. What did these moments teach you about your strengths?

Write these examples down, not just as achievements but as evidence of your ability to create solutions and drive outcomes. These moments become the foundation of the entrepreneurial narrative you're creating and help you articulate your value to clients and collaborators.

Embracing Your "Boss" Mindset

Let's talk about the mindset you'll need to move forward. Many high-achieving women enter new spaces, such as entrepreneurship, and downplay their skills because it feels like "starting over." But here's the truth: you aren't starting over; you're building on your strengths.

Consider the times in your career when you've had to take charge, make tough decisions, and get results. This same "boss" mentality is what will help you succeed as an entrepreneur. Remember, if you could do it there, you can do it here. Success doesn't come from a title; it comes from your mindset, your strategy, and your resilience.

To reinforce this mentality, adopt practices that remind you of your leadership ability. Create a mantra around leadership that you use to set the tone for your day. Let those words remind you of exactly who you are whenever you're facing a situation that shakes your confidence as a CEO.

Find and Own Your Unique Value

Market Value vs. Job Description

As an employee, your value is often measured by your ability to perform a specific job description. However, your market value goes beyond those limits. As an entrepreneur, your market value is the full package of knowledge, skills, experience, and excellence you bring to the table, the problems you can solve, and the perspective you offer.

Exercise: Write a list of your achievements that go beyond the scope of any job title you've held. Then, describe what problem you solved or what positive impact you created in each situation. Think of these as the "seeds" of your entrepreneurial value. You'll quickly see that your experience has multiple layers of value, each of which is needed and marketable.

Expanding Beyond the Resume

To elevate this practice, think about the intangible aspects of your career. Have you built relationships that led to business growth or navigated challenging team dynamics to achieve success? These often-overlooked accomplishments add depth to your market value. Document these examples and revisit them to remind yourself of how multidimensional your strengths and your value are.

Mindset Shift Exercise: Redefining Yourself as a Product

To step more deeply into this mindset, think of your expertise as a product that can serve others. What do you bring that no one else does? What's the unique value you provide? Take time with these questions, writing down your responses as they come to you. This exercise will help you see yourself as a provider of solutions, a thought leader, and a creator of value; all of which are key attributes of a successful entrepreneur.

Fuel Your Confidence to Lead Like a CEO

Building Inner Confidence for the Next Level

If you've been successful in your career, you already know how confidence changes everything. Still, stepping into the role of CEO may challenge your confidence in ways you haven't faced before. This is when it becomes essential to internalize that being a CEO is simply the next evolution of your leadership.

As a daily practice, begin affirming your readiness to lead. You might start with simple affirmations like:

- I am ready to lead my business with confidence and clarity.
- I bring a wealth of knowledge and experience that adds real value to my business.
- My success as a CEO is a natural extension of my past achievements.

Affirmations and visualizations help reinforce your mindset, and make it easier to navigate challenges through your self-belief. Each time you affirm your own power and readiness, you reinforce your confidence and lay the groundwork for authentic leadership that will lead your business to success.

Self-Belief Anchors

Think back on moments when you felt most accomplished or recognized in your career. These experiences are your "self-belief anchors," and they'll remind you of your capabilities when self-doubt begins to creep in. Choose a few of these milestones, write them down, and place them somewhere you can see every day. Let them be a reminder of who you are and why you're more than ready to be a CEO.

Developing Your CEO Habits

Confidence isn't just a mindset; it's also about habits that reflect leadership. Start building routines that align with your CEO role. This might include setting aside time for strategic thinking, networking with like-minded leaders, or carving out moments for reflection and planning. These habits reinforce your readiness to lead and are tangible steps toward the fulfillment of your vision.

Embarking on Your CEO Journey with Confidence

You're more than ready to build a business that reflects your ambition, purpose, and values. This mindset isn't just about creating a new career; it's about stepping fully into your power as a leader.

As you move through the next chapters, keep returning to the qualities that have contributed to your success this far: resilience, intelligence, and vision, etc. With the right mindset, you're not only breaking through; you're creating something entirely new.

The path to entrepreneurship is as much a journey of self-discovery as it is a professional endeavor. So take a deep breath, embrace your strengths, and get ready to lead in a way you never have before.

2

Focus on the Endgame: Building a Purpose-Driven Business Aligned with Your Life

Defining Your Why and Your Vision

Many people dream of owning a business, but not everyone is intentional about why they're starting one. A business that brings real fulfillment is born out of purpose and aligns with the life you want to live. This chapter will guide you to define your vision and understand the critical role that alignment plays in building a business that supports, rather than disrupts, the life you envision.

If you're here, it's because you want a business that allows you to thrive personally, professionally, and purposefully. This chapter will help you get clear about what that looks like.

Frame Your Vision and Purpose

Your Vision for Life and Work

Before setting goals for your business, take time to reflect on the life you want. What do you see when you picture a fulfilled life? Imagine the freedom, flexibility, and purpose you desire. These aspirations should shape your business, guiding every decision from whom you serve to how you operate.

Exercise: Write down answers to these questions to clarify your vision:

- What does an ideal workday look like for me?
- How do I want my business to fit into my personal life?
- What values are non-negotiable for me as a business owner?

Expanding Your Vision

Take your reflections a step further by envisioning your legacy. Beyond immediate goals, what impact do you want your business to have on your community, your family, or your industry? This long-term perspective will help you build a business that's not only aligned with your current and desired lifestyle but also capable of evolving as your vision grows.

Discovering and Embracing Your Purpose

Purpose goes beyond profit; it's what fuels your business and keeps you connected to why you started in the first place.

When your business aligns with your calling, it will feel less like "work" and more like the thing you were born to do.

Exercise: Reflect on what called you to start this business. Consider these questions:

- What positive change do I want to create?
- What problems do I feel uniquely equipped to solve?
- How can my business be a reflection of my values and calling?

By getting in touch with your purpose, you ensure your business remains aligned with what genuinely matters to you; even as you face the inevitable challenges of entrepreneurship.

Fit Your Business to Your Lifestyle

Lifestyle by Design, Not Default

One of the greatest advantages of entrepreneurship is the freedom to shape your work around your life, instead of the other way around. The lifestyle you want should inform your business model, workload, and daily structure. Many entrepreneurs fall into the trap of working harder than they ever did in a job. This section will guide you on how to avoid that.

Visualize the different areas of your life: family, friends, spirituality, self-care, community involvement, etc. How do you want to show up in each area? Then, think about how your business can support this vision, rather than compete with it.

Expanding the Design Process

Building a lifestyle-aligned business requires honesty about your priorities. Are there areas where you've been compromising in your current role? What small changes could you make to avoid this in your business? Document these thoughts and revisit them as you plan.

Designing Your Freedom Framework

Your "freedom framework" is the unique structure that allows you to prioritize what matters most. Whether it's the flexibility to attend family events, pursue creative interests, or engage in community service, this framework will guide your choices in how you set up and run your business.

Exercise: Answer these key questions to build your framework:

- How many hours a week do I want to dedicate to my business?
- What boundaries do I need to put in place to protect my time and energy?
- What processes and support do I need to sustain this lifestyle as my business grows?

Implementing Your Framework

Once you've defined your freedom framework, consider the steps to make it a reality. For example, could you outsource administrative tasks to free up more time? Could you automate parts of your business to reduce your workload? This step ensures your framework isn't just a vision but a plan you can put into action.

Forge Alignment Between Business and Life

Setting Goals with Intentionality

Traditional goal-setting often prioritizes growth at all costs, but for a business aligned with purpose, growth should be intentional. Setting business goals that align with your life vision ensures that success doesn't come at the expense of what matters most to you.

Here are some ways to set goals intentionally:

- Prioritize alignment over achievement: Choose goals that bring you closer to the life you want, not just higher numbers.

- Plan for sustainability: Build your goals around what is sustainable and realistic for you.

- Measure success in more than one way: While revenue is essential, also measure success in terms of fulfillment, balance, and impact.

Creating a Balance Between Ambition and Lifestyle

Ambition is valuable, but it should serve, not overshadow, your ideal lifestyle. This section will guide you to align your drive for success with lifestyle considerations. Success in business can only be sustainable when it's built on a foundation of alignment.

Consider your current commitments and energy. As you establish business goals, think about how each will affect your ability to show up fully in the areas that matter most to you. This focus on alignment will allow you to enjoy both your work and personal life.

Expanding Alignment Practices

Incorporate regular check-ins with yourself to ensure you're staying aligned. These could be monthly reflections on what's working and what's not or quarterly reviews of your goals and how they align with your vision. Consistency in these practices will help you make adjustments before misalignment becomes a problem.

Building Your Business with Alignment at the Core

Every decision you make while building your business should serve the vision you have for your life. You're creating something meaningful, not just a paycheck, and that requires clarity and intention. Your business should be a vehicle that propels you toward a fulfilling life, not one that pulls you away from it.

Take time now to revisit the reflections and exercises in this chapter. Look for ways to stay true to your vision and to protect your boundaries as you build. You're creating a business that doesn't just build your bank account; it supports, uplifts, and fulfills every aspect of who you are.

3

Find Your Tribe: The Power of Community on the Entrepreneurial Journey

From Independent Leader to Supported Visionary

In your career and life, you've likely been the person others turn to for support, guidance, and strength. You've been the rock, the mentor, the advisor. But entrepreneurship is a different path. It's one that requires leaning on others just as much as giving support. It's easy to assume you'll navigate this journey on your own, but there is immense power in building a community around you.

Starting a business can feel isolating, especially for Black women who often face unique challenges and limited representation. By connecting with a community of like-minded entrepreneurs, you create a circle of support, a safe space to share openly, and a wellspring of ideas and encouragement. This chapter will guide you in shifting from independent leader to supported visionary.

Foster Connection in Your Entrepreneurial Journey

Overcoming the Myth of the "Solopreneur"

Society and social media often celebrate the image of a solo entrepreneur who singlehandedly "makes it," but in reality, the most successful entrepreneurs surround themselves with the right people. In entrepreneurship, you'll face situations and challenges that aren't easily overcome alone. Knowing that others are walking a similar path can make all the difference in your commitment and success.

This section encourages you to reframe support as a necessity, not a luxury. Here are a few areas where community makes entrepreneurship easier:

- **Problem-Solving**: Challenges are easier to address when you have access to the experiences and solutions of others.

- **Resource Sharing**: Access to a wider network means access to tools, advice, and opportunities that you may not find when you keep to yourself.

- **Emotional Support**: Having people who understand the highs and lows of entrepreneurship will help you through the tough times.

Exercise: Reflect on a recent challenge you faced in your business or career. How might having access to a supportive community have changed the outcome? Write down specific ways others could have provided insight, solutions, or encouragement.

Your Network as a Growth Engine

As an entrepreneur, your network is more than just a safety net. It's an engine for growth, bringing fresh ideas, perspectives, and connections that move your business forward. Community isn't just about emotional support; it's a source of resources that can advance your success in unexpected ways.

Exercise: Reflect on the types of support that would make the biggest difference for you:

- Where do I feel least confident in my business right now?
- What expertise or advice would I like access to?
- What kind of encouragement or camaraderie would make this journey more enjoyable?

These questions can help you define the type of community you need as you move forward.

Find the Right People to Support You

Creating Intentional Connections

Finding your community starts with intentional outreach and open-mindedness. Seek out spaces specifically designed for Black women entrepreneurs, where shared experience fosters a sense of safety, camaraderie, and support. Whether through online communities, local meetups, or mastermind groups, creating intentional connections can help you build a support system that understands and amplifies your unique journey.

Exercise: Reflect on what you most want in a community:

- Do I want ongoing accountability and check-ins?
- Am I looking for business advice, emotional support, or both?
- How often do I want to engage with this community?

Answering these questions can help you find a group that fits your needs and goals.

Learning from Others Who Have Been There

A community is also a powerful resource for knowledge. In spaces dedicated to Black women entrepreneurs, you'll find peers who have already overcome some of the challenges you may face. By learning from their experiences, you gain insight, avoid common pitfalls, and feel empowered by their progress and success.

Exercise: Consider these questions as you seek advice or inspiration from others in the community:

- What are common challenges they've faced and how did they overcome them?
- What tools, processes, or strategies have been most effective for them?
- What lessons or insights have they gained that would apply to my journey?

When you connect with others who have "been there," you not only learn from their experiences but you also gain the reassurance that success is possible.

Form Your Circle of Strength

The Power of Collective Accountability

Entrepreneurship requires accountability, and being part of a supportive circle can help keep you on track. By sharing goals, celebrating wins, and discussing challenges with others, you hold yourself to a higher standard and receive feedback that can accelerate your growth. You don't have to shoulder it all alone; a strong community will help you move forward, step by step.

Think about the goals you would benefit from sharing with a community. Then, consider setting up regular check-ins with trusted peers or a mentor to ensure that you stay aligned and motivated. This collective accountability transforms solo goals into shared milestones and will make your journey more rewarding.

Creating a Space for Honest, Vulnerable Conversations

One of the greatest gifts of community is having a safe space to share openly and vulnerably. In entrepreneurship, frustrations, fears, and self-doubt are all part of the journey, but you don't have to face them in isolation. A supportive group allows you to be honest about the struggles, making it easier to keep going.

If you haven't yet, seek out groups or individuals you feel safe opening up with, where you can be both honest and uplifted. When challenges arise, let this be the place where you share them, find advice, and connect with those who understand.

Over time, these relationships can evolve into trusted partnerships that provide ongoing strength and encouragement.

Step into Community and Let It Support You

No one builds something massive or meaningful alone. As you start or continue your entrepreneurial journey, remember that support is a strength, not a weakness. Leaning on a community isn't just about making your journey easier; it's about enriching your experience with resources, insights, and connections that can save you time, money, and energy while moving you forward.

Make a commitment to build and nurture the relationships that will support and strengthen you as you grow. Together, we can break barriers, create legacies, and make an impact that goes beyond our individual businesses.

4

Fortify for the Future: Creating Lasting Success by Embracing Incremental Growth

---

Embracing Patience and Progress

When you have a big vision, it's natural to feel eager to bring it to life. But building something meaningful and sustainable takes time. Trying to accomplish everything in your first launch is a fast track to burnout. Instead, imagine your business as a journey of intentional steps that build a foundation for long-term success.

In this chapter, we'll explore the art of growing incrementally and embracing small, strategic steps that bring your vision to life over time. You'll learn to focus on progress, not perfection, and create a business that's strong, adaptable, and ready to scale when the time is right.

Focus on Building a Strong Foundation

The Importance of Starting Small and Growing Steadily

Launching a business is like building a house: without a solid foundation, it won't stand for long. Many new entrepreneurs want to do it all: offering multiple services, expanding rapidly, or marketing across every platform. But sustainable growth starts with a focused foundation, allowing you to build something stable that supports your larger vision over time.

Exercise: Reflect on your vision and ask yourself:

- What is the core mission of my business?
- What is one main offer I can focus on at launch that embodies this mission?
- What small goals can I set that align with my long-term vision?

Each of these questions will help you narrow down what matters most at the beginning, ensuring that every step you take is purposeful and aligned.

Identifying Your Minimum Viable Product (MVP)

In the startup world, a minimum viable product (MVP) is a basic version of an offering designed to test its value and gather feedback. Your MVP allows you to launch sooner, learn from your audience, and refine your business without feeling overwhelmed by the pressure to make it perfect on the first try.

Think of your MVP as the simplest, most valuable version of your service or product that still delivers real results. For example, if your goal is to provide coaching, perhaps start with a single, focused coaching package instead of launching multiple programs. Once you have feedback and success stories, you can expand naturally.

Exercise: Identify what your MVP might look like. Write down the core components of your offer and how it addresses your audience's immediate needs. What steps can you take to launch this MVP within the next 30-90 days?

Form Realistic and Actionable Goals

Establishing Milestones, Not Mountains

Instead of trying to climb a mountain all at once, create smaller, manageable milestones that bring you closer to your vision without overwhelming you. Each milestone represents a step forward, makes the process feel achievable and encourages you to celebrate your progress.

   Exercise: Start by breaking down your big vision into these smaller steps:

1. What's one short-term goal I can achieve within the next month?
2. What steps can I take this quarter that move me toward my bigger vision?
3. How can I pace myself to ensure I don't burn out?

   By focusing on incremental goals, you're able to see measurable progress without the pressure to do everything immediately.

Planning for Long-Term Scalability

The beauty of growing one step at a time is that it allows for sustainable, intentional, and aligned expansion. As you meet your milestones, you're in a position to decide which aspects of your business to expand next, based on what's working and what your audience needs. You're building something that isn't just profitable but adaptable and positioned to scale.

As you move forward, keep your long-term vision in mind, but allow it to unfold naturally. This approach will keep your goals aligned with your purpose and avoid the common pitfall of growing too quickly without the foundation to support it or growing something you hate.

Tip: Regularly review your progress and assess your scalability. Are there processes you can streamline or automate to support sustainable growth?

Follow the Process and Stay the Course

Learning to Love Incremental Wins

It's easy to become so focused on the end goal that we overlook the smaller wins along the way. Celebrating incremental wins fuels your momentum and reinforces that you're on the right path.

Exercise: Reflect on each small win as proof that you're making progress:

- What were my top three wins this week?
- How did each step bring me closer to my larger vision?

- What did I learn from this progress that I can apply moving forward?

By acknowledging each accomplishment, you'll create a positive cycle of motivation and gratitude that inspires you to keep building.

Overcoming the Pressure for Instant Results

In a world where overnight success stories dominate the headlines, it's natural to feel pressure to see results immediately. But real success is often quieter, growing over time through consistency, resilience, and intentional choices. Remember, building an empire isn't a race; it's a journey that unfolds in its own time.

Create a mantra or affirmation to remind yourself of the value of incremental growth. For example:

- "Every step I take is building a strong, purpose-driven business."
- "Progress, not perfection, is my path to success."

Repeat this mantra whenever you feel the urge to rush or compare your progress to others. Trust that each step is bringing you closer to your vision.

Exercise: Write down one area where you feel pressure to achieve instant results. Identify three small steps you can take today to make progress in that area without overwhelming yourself.

Building Your Vision, One Step at a Time

Your vision is big, bold, and beautiful. But remember, even the smallest of empires weren't built overnight. As you take intentional, purposeful steps toward your dream, trust that you are building something impactful and enduring.

Commit to pacing yourself, celebrate each milestone, and focus on the journey rather than the destination. The process of growing one step at a time doesn't just lead to success; it leads to a business that reflects your purpose, your values, and the legacy you're here to create.

Tip: Keep a journal of your milestones and reflections. Over time, this record will become a powerful reminder of your progress and the foundation you've built for your future.

5

Follow a Framework: Commit to Your Path and Let It Work

The Power of Consistency and Commitment

When you're starting a business, the number of strategies, opinions, and "must-try" methods can feel overwhelming. One expert tells you to focus on social media, another recommends webinars, and yet another says email marketing is the key. But the truth is, success doesn't come from trying everything; it comes from following one proven process with commitment, focus, and patience.

In this chapter, we'll discuss why choosing a structured path and sticking to it is critical for sustainable growth. You'll learn the value of giving a chosen process time to work, and how trusting the steps you've committed to can lead to lasting success.

Following a Proven Process Matters

Avoiding the Trap of Constantly Shifting Tactics

It's tempting to switch gears every time a new strategy or attractive opportunity arises. But constantly jumping from one approach to another will dilute your efforts, waste time, and lead to burnout. Instead, by choosing a proven process, you focus your energy on executing a series of steps that have been designed and tested to yield results.

Exercise: Reflect on past projects or goals:

- What strategies have I abandoned too soon in the past?
- How could my efforts have turned out differently if I had committed fully to one path?
- What changes could I see in my business if I gave a chosen process the time to work?

Learning to trust the process you've chosen will help you channel your energy, eliminate distractions, and build with clarity.

Embracing Process Over Perfection

Choosing one process doesn't mean things will be perfect right away, but it does mean you'll move forward consistently. A proven process is designed with your success in mind, so don't let small setbacks or imperfections tempt you to abandon it. Each step is a part of the bigger picture, even if the progress feels slight.

Give yourself permission to trust that following the process will ultimately yield more than sporadic efforts in different directions. Commit to showing up consistently, knowing that each step is bringing you closer to your goal.

Giving the Process Time to Work

Why Commitment is Key

Following a process requires patience and discipline. Results often compound over time. You might not see immediate progress, but consistent effort will build momentum. Trusting each step and giving it time to produce results is essential to your success.

When you're tempted to jump ahead or switch approaches, remember:

- Processes and frameworks are designed with long-term results in mind.
- Success often follows consistency, even through slower seasons.
- Each small action contributes to the larger vision.

Exercise: Reflect on these questions as you commit to your chosen framework:

- Am I giving each step the time and focus it needs?
- How can I better trust the process I've committed to?
- What specific goals do I want to see accomplished by staying true to this process?

Remember, results take time. Recognize that your success story will be no less powerful because it took time; in fact, it will be more rewarding.

Fight the Urge to Pivot Prematurely

The Myth of Overnight Success

Sustainable success is rarely achieved overnight. Most successful entrepreneurs have spent years laying a foundation, often working behind the scenes to build something that will last.

Staying Consistent Through the Slow Seasons

Every process has seasons, some more fruitful than others. In the slower times, it's common to feel doubt or frustration, but these are the times when consistency matters most. Use these seasons as an opportunity to refine your skills, evaluate what you're learning, and build the resilience needed to reach your goals.

Some ways to stay consistent during slower seasons:

- Revisit your original vision and goals.
- Remind yourself of the milestones you've already achieved.
- Celebrate the small wins that reflect progress, even if they feel insignficant.

By staying consistent, you're preparing yourself for the times when growth accelerates. You'll be ready to handle the challenges and opportunities that come with that acceleration.

Commit to the Path and Reap the Rewards

Success doesn't come from trying everything; it comes from doing the right things consistently over time. As you move forward, trust the process you've chosen and commit fully to it. Give each step the time it needs, and focus on executing with patience, discipline, and faith in the outcome.

If you're tempted to abandon your process, pause, reflect on your "why," and remember that each step you take is a step closer to your dream. The path may be long, but every successful entrepreneur was once where you are now, facing challenges, growing, and building something worth the journey.

Tip: Keep a journal of your journey through the framework. Document wins, setbacks, and lessons learned. This journal will become a testament to your growth and the power of commitment and consistency.

6

Forge Your Exit Strategy: Paving the Way for a Confident Transition to Full-Time Entrepreneurship

Embracing a Vision for Your Future

You're on the path to building a business that aligns with your purpose, values, and lifestyle. Now, it's time to consider how you'll eventually transition from your current job to full-time entrepreneurship. This isn't about leaving on a whim; it's about creating a plan that sets you up for success. A well-planned exit strategy provides a roadmap, ensuring that when the time comes, you're confident, financially prepared, and equipped for what lies ahead.

In this chapter, we'll explore how to identify what you need in place to leave your job, establish a realistic timeline, and plan the steps that will empower you to make a smooth and successful exit.

Find Clarity on What You Need Before You Leave

Financial Readiness: Creating a Safety Net

One of the most crucial parts of an exit strategy is ensuring you have a financial cushion in place. Entrepreneurship can come with unpredictable income and expenses, especially in the early stages, so having a safety net will provide peace of mind and allow you to focus on growth rather than survival.

Exercise: Reflect on your financial goals and responsibilities:

- What are my monthly expenses, including both personal and business costs?
- How much money do I want saved as a cushion before I leave my job?
- What revenue milestones do I want my business to reach before I transition?

Setting financial targets will give you a clear sense of when it's the right time to make your exit and prevent the stress of financial instability during your first months as a full-time entrepreneur.

Exercise: Calculate your current monthly expenses and set a savings goal for a 6-9 month safety net. Outline the specific steps you need to take to reach this goal within your timeline.

Building a Sustainable Revenue Stream

Before leaving your job, aim to establish at least one reliable source of income within your business. This could be a product, service, or client base that generates consistent revenue. Knowing that your business is already earning will give you confidence and stability as you step away from the security of a paycheck.

Exercise: Consider these questions as you assess your revenue stream:

- What's the minimum revenue goal that would allow me to cover essential expenses?
- What additional income goals would provide comfort and flexibility?
- How can I optimize my offers to make income more predictable?

Tip: Focus on recurring revenue streams, such as subscription-based services or retainers, to create more financial stability. Document your monthly income trends to evaluate your progress.

By focusing on revenue consistency, you're laying the groundwork for a sustainable and successful transition.

Formulate a Realistic Timeline for Transition

Setting Your Exit Date with Flexibility

Choosing a target date to leave your job is empowering. It gives you a concrete goal to work toward and allows you to align your business efforts with that goal. However, it's essential to maintain flexibility and give yourself permission to adjust this date based on progress or unexpected challenges.

Exercise: Ask yourself:

- What feels like a reasonable timeline to reach my exit goals?

- Do I want to transition gradually by reducing hours at my job if possible?
- How will I know if I need to extend my timeline to meet my financial or revenue goals?

Planning a flexible timeline allows you to work toward your exit date with purpose while staying realistic and open to adjustments.

Mapping Key Milestones on the Way to Exit

To create a smooth transition, break down your timeline into smaller milestones. These could include financial targets, business goals, and skill-building objectives. Mapping milestones helps you stay organized and motivated as you work toward your goal.

Examples of exit milestones might include:

- Saving a designated amount in a business/emergency fund.
- Consistently earning a target revenue level for at least three consecutive months.
- Building out core systems in your business to handle client work smoothly.

Exercise: Create a milestone map with dates and specific goals for each milestone. Track your progress monthly and adjust your efforts to stay on schedule.

This milestone map will give you a clear view of your progress and keep you on track as you work toward your exit date.

Fortify Your Business for Full-Time Success

Creating Systems to Support Growth

When you leave your job, your business will become your primary focus. It's essential to have systems in place to handle increased demands efficiently. These might include automating tasks, refining your sales process, or establishing workflows for delivering your products or services. Solid systems will enable you to scale your business confidently once you're in it full-time.

Exercise: Think about the areas of your business that will need support:

- Which tasks can I automate or delegate to free up my time?
- How can I create processes that streamline my workflow?
- What tools or resources can support my business operations as they grow?

Tip: Start small by automating repetitive tasks like email, scheduling, or invoicing. Test tools like CRM platforms or project management software to enhance your efficiency.

Setting up these systems before your transition will make your business more manageable, freeing you to focus on growth and client relationships.

Identifying the Support You Need

Leaving your job to become a full-time entrepreneur can feel like stepping into the unknown, but having support will ease the transition. This support might include a coach, peers in your field, an established framework, a process, or a plan to follow.

Exercise: Consider what kind of support you'll need most:

- Do I need accountability to stay on track with my goals?
- Am I looking for guidance in specific business areas, like marketing or client acquisition?
- What type of support is best for me, group, one-on-one, or Done For You?

Take Your Next Step Toward Freedom

Creating a plan to leave your job isn't just about ending one chapter; it's about fully stepping into the life you've envisioned. By focusing on financial readiness, establishing a timeline, and preparing your business for growth, you're setting yourself up for a confident, empowered transition.

Take time to map out your exit strategy, envision your future, and put practical steps in place to reach your goals. Remember, every milestone you reach brings you one step closer to becoming the full-time CEO of your purpose-driven business. You've prepared, committed, and built with intention; now, it's time to step boldly toward your dream.

Tip: Keep a journal of your exit strategy journey. Document your milestones, reflections, and lessons learned to serve as a source of inspiration and a roadmap for others you may help in the future.

PART 2:

The Framework

1

Follow the Framework: Introducing the Ready to Launch Framework

A Roadmap to Purpose-Driven and Aligned Success

Building a business from the ground up can feel overwhelming. There are countless strategies, tools, and opinions to navigate, leaving many aspiring entrepreneurs unsure of where to start. That's where the *Ready to Launch Framework* comes in. This is a step-by-step process designed to guide you through creating a business that's aligned with your purpose, profitable, and built to thrive.

This chapter introduces the framework as a proven system to eliminate the guesswork and confusion that often comes with launching a business. It's tailored specifically for aspiring and emerging entrepreneurs who are ready to transition from idea to income with clarity, confidence, and alignment.

Why a Framework Matters

Many entrepreneurs struggle to launch successfully because they lack structure. They jump from one idea to the next or try to follow piecemeal advice that doesn't fit their unique goals. The result? Burnout, wasted time, and businesses that fail to gain traction.

The **Ready to Launch Framework** offers a clear and intentional approach to avoid these pitfalls. By breaking the process into manageable phases, it ensures you:

- Stay focused on the right priorities at the right time.
- Build your business on a solid foundation aligned with your values.
- Progress step by step without feeling overwhelmed.
- Gain confidence in your decisions and execution.

This framework isn't just about creating a business; it's about creating a business that reflects who you are and the impact you want to make.

Overview of the Five Phases

The **Ready to Launch Framework** is structured into five distinct phases, each addressing a critical aspect of building and launching a purposeful and aligned business. Here's a high-level overview:

1. **Preparation**: Build the foundation by defining your vision, shifting your mindset, and aligning your goals with your core values.

2. **Positioning**: Identify your target audience, carve out your niche, and create a unique value proposition that sets you apart.

3. **Packaging**: Design a compelling offer that meets your audience's needs, aligns with your financial goals, and is ready to deliver results.

4. **Planning**: Develop marketing and sales strategies to attract and convert your ideal clients while building systems for scalability.

5. **Promotion**: Execute your launch with confidence, engage with your audience, and set the stage for sustainable growth.

Each phase builds on the last, creating a seamless flow from ideation to execution. Together, they provide a comprehensive roadmap to ensure no essential steps are missed.

What Sets the Ready to Launch Framework Apart

While many business frameworks focus solely on profitability, the *Ready to Launch Framework* emphasizes alignment and purpose. It's designed for entrepreneurs who want to build businesses that not only generate income but also reflect their values and support their desired lifestyle. Key differentiators include:

- **Alignment**: Each phase ensures your business aligns with your vision and values, so you're building something impactful and authentic.

- **Clarity**: The framework simplifies complex decisions, offering clear steps and strategies to guide you forward.
- **Sustainability**: By emphasizing foundational work and incremental growth, the framework helps you create a business that's built to last.
- **Support**: Whether you're navigating mindset shifts or marketing plans, the framework provides tools, resources, and a community to support your journey.

How to Approach the Framework

The beauty of the *Ready to Launch Framework* lies in its flexibility. While the phases are designed to be followed sequentially, you can revisit and refine each step as your business evolves. Here's how to approach it:

1. **Commit to the Process**: Trust the framework and give each phase the time and focus it deserves.
2. **Personalize Your Journey**: Adapt the steps to fit your unique goals, business, and strengths.
3. **Stay Open to Growth**: Allow yourself to learn and adjust as you go, knowing that entrepreneurship is a dynamic experience.

By embracing the framework, you'll not only gain clarity and direction but also develop the confidence to lead your business with purpose.

Your Next Steps

In the chapters ahead, we'll take a deep dive into each phase of the framework, starting with **Preparation**. You'll learn how to establish a strong foundation for your business by defining your vision, aligning with your values, and adopting a CEO mindset.

As you read, remember: this framework is more than a guide; it's a partnership in your entrepreneurial journey. You're not alone in this process, and with the *Ready to Launch Framework*, you have the tools to build a business that reflects your brilliance and creates lasting impact.

Are you ready to launch? Let's get started.

2

Firm Up Your Foundation: Preparation for Business Success

The Importance of Preparation

Every successful business begins with a strong foundation. Just as a well-built house requires careful planning and a solid base, your business needs clarity, alignment, and intention before you take your first big steps. The **Preparation** phase of the *Ready to Launch Framework* focuses on ensuring your business aligns with your mission, vision, and values while equipping you with the mindset to thrive as a CEO. This is where transformation begins.

By the end of this phase, you will have:

- A clear sense of your business mission and vision.
- Goals that align with your values and desired lifestyle.

- Tools to confront and overcome limiting beliefs.
- Confidence in your role as a CEO.
- A defined understanding of your unique impact.

Mission, Vision, Goals, and Values

Crafting Your Mission Statement

Your mission statement answers the question: **Why does my business exist?** It's your guiding purpose; the reason you're stepping into entrepreneurship. A strong mission reflects your core beliefs and serves as a north star, keeping you grounded when challenges arise and providing direction when facing tough decisions.

Exercise: Write a one-sentence mission statement that answers:

- What problem does my business solve?
- Who does it serve?
- Why does it matter?

Example: "My mission is to empower Black women entrepreneurs to build aligned, profitable businesses that support their purpose and lifestyle."

Envisioning Your Future

Your vision statement paints a picture of what you want to achieve. It's aspirational, describing the long-term impact your business will create. A clear vision helps you stay motivated and make decisions that align with your goals.

Exercise: Imagine your ideal business five years from now. What does it look like? Who are you helping? What's the impact?

- Write down three specific outcomes you want to see.
- Use these to craft a vision statement that inspires you.

Setting Goals That Align With Your Values

Your goals translate your mission and vision into actionable steps. However, it's essential that these goals align with your core values to ensure your business feels authentic and sustainable.

In the ***Ready to Launch Incubator***, we guide you through a process to determine your 12-month personal and business goals, your top three to five values, and ensure alignment between your goals and values.

Exercise: Reflect on:

- What are my short-term and long-term goals?
- How do these goals reflect what matters most to me?
- What steps will I take this month to move closer to these goals?

Limiting Beliefs and Mindset

Confronting Limiting Beliefs

Many entrepreneurs face internal blocks: fears, doubts, and beliefs that undermine their confidence. To prepare for success, you must identify and challenge these limiting beliefs.

Common limiting beliefs show up in thoughts, statements, and questions that sound like:

- "I'm not ready to start my own business."
- "I'll never make as much money as I did in my job."
- "What if I fail?"

Exercise: Write down one belief that's holding you back. Then, reframe it into an empowering statement.

- Limiting Belief: "I don't have enough experience to be successful."
- Reframed: "My career experience has equipped me with the skills I need to succeed."

Cultivating a Growth-Oriented Mindset

Success begins in your mind. A growth mindset embraces challenges, sees failures as opportunities, and celebrates progress over perfection. In the ***Ready to Launch Incubator***, tools like the *Limiting Beliefs Masterclass* guide you in shifting from self-doubt to self-belief.

Exercise: Practice daily affirmations to reinforce your confidence:

- "I am ready to lead my business with purpose and clarity."
- "Every step I take brings me closer to my vision."
- "I have the skills, knowledge, and resilience to succeed."

Becoming a CEO

Embracing Your CEO Identity

Transitioning from employee to entrepreneur requires a shift in identity. As a CEO, you're not just building a business; you're leading it. This means making strategic decisions, setting boundaries, and stepping fully into your power.

Exercise: What does being a CEO mean to you? Write down three qualities you admire in leaders and how you'll embody them in your business.

Building Confidence as a Leader

Leadership is a skill you grow into (you've done a lot of this work already), and confidence comes with practice. Start by celebrating small wins and learning from each decision you make. Exercises like the **B.O.S.S. CEO Mantra** in *Ready to Launch* help you define and communicate the type of leader you are.

Tip: Schedule a weekly "CEO Day" to plan, strategize, and review your goals. This dedicated time reinforces your role as the leader of your business.

Determining Your IMPACT

Your business has the potential to create meaningful change, both for your clients and yourself. Our IMPACT framework helps you define:

- **I**: The *Intent* behind your business.

- **M**: The *Mission* it seeks to accomplish through its products and services.
- **P**: Your *Power;* the qualities and experiences that distinguish you from other people doing similar work.
- **A**: Your *A-Game;* the primary result your products and services deliver.
- **C**: The *Change Process;* how you deliver your results.
- **T**: The *Transformation* your products and services create.

Your Path Forward

The Preparation phase is about more than solidifying a strong foundation; it's about stepping into your power as a visionary leader. By defining your mission, vision, goals, and values, confronting limiting beliefs, and embracing your CEO identity, you're creating a business that's not only profitable but deeply aligned with who you are.

With these tools and practices, you're ready to move to the next phase: **Positioning**. Here, you'll define your ideal audience and carve out a unique space in the market.

3

Focus Your Niche: Positioning Yourself to Stand Out

The Power of Positioning

In a crowded marketplace, simply having a great idea or a solid business plan isn't enough. To succeed, you must stand out and speak directly to the people who need your solutions the most. Positioning is about defining your space in the market; a space where your unique voice, skills, and offers shine. It's not about trying to reach everyone; it's about connecting deeply with the right ones.

This phase is your opportunity to embrace what makes you different and use it to carve out a niche that aligns with your values and serves your ideal clients. By the end of this chapter, you'll have clarity on who you're serving, the transformation you're offering, and why you're uniquely equipped to deliver it.

Defining Your Ideal Client

Understanding Who You Serve

Your ideal client is more than just a demographic. They are the people who resonate with your message, value your expertise, and are ready to invest in the transformation you provide. Identifying them with precision allows you to craft offers and messaging that speak directly to their hearts.

Exercise: Ask yourself:

- Who are the people I feel called to serve?
- What specific challenges or pain points do they face?
- How does my experience position me to help them?

Exercise: Picture your dream client. Write a short story about their life, their struggles, and how your business changes their trajectory. Give them a name, personality traits, and a vision of success that you can help them achieve.

In the ***Ready to Launch Incubator***, we use the **Power Portrait** exercise to go deeper into identifying your client's pain points, desires, and decision-making triggers. This tool helps refine your messaging for maximum connection.

Speaking Directly to Their Pain Points

When you understand your ideal client's pain points and desires, you can create messaging that makes them feel seen, heard, and understood. This connection builds trust and positions you as the solution they've been seeking.

Tip: Use empathetic language in your messaging. Instead of saying, "I offer business coaching," try, "I help medical professionals turn their skills into profitable businesses they love."

Narrowing Your Niche

The Freedom of Focus

It's tempting to try to serve everyone, but the truth is that your impact grows when you narrow your focus. By specializing in a specific niche, you become the go-to expert for a particular audience or need. This not only simplifies your marketing but also strengthens your ability to deliver exceptional results.

Exercise: What problem do I solve better than anyone else? How can I refine my focus to serve those who need that solution most?

Embracing Your Expertise

Your niche should align with your strengths and passions. Think about your unique skills, life experiences, and professional expertise. These are the building blocks of your niche; the areas where you can create the most value and stand out from the crowd.

Conducting Market Research

Understanding Your Competition

Market research isn't about comparison; it's about understanding the landscape. By analyzing competitors, you can identify gaps in the market and opportunities to differentiate yourself.

Ask yourself:

- What are my competitors doing well?
- Where are they falling short?
- How can I position myself to fill those gaps?

Listening to Your Audience

Your ideal clients are the best source of insights. Engage with them to learn about their needs, preferences, and challenges. Use surveys, interviews, or social media interactions to gather valuable data.

Tip: Join online communities or groups where your ideal clients hang out. Pay attention to their questions, frustrations, and aspirations to refine your offers and messaging.

Crafting Your Unique Selling Proposition (USP)

What Sets You Apart

Your USP is the core of your positioning. It's the statement that explains what makes you different and why clients should choose you over others. Writing a compelling USP requires clarity, confidence, and a deep understanding of your audience's needs.

Formula for a Strong USP:

- **Who you help**: Identify your audience.
- **What you do**: Highlight the transformation you provide.

- **Why it matters**: Explain the unique value or impact of your solution.

Example: "I help Black women professionals turn their expertise into purpose-driven businesses, so they can achieve financial freedom and make a meaningful impact."

Aligning Your USP with Your Mission

Your USP should reflect your mission and values, ensuring that every aspect of your business communicates a cohesive and authentic message.

Exercise: Write your USP using the formula above. Then, ask yourself: Does this statement align with my mission? Does it resonate with the audience I want to serve?

In the ***Ready to Launch Incubator***, we guide you through crafting and refining your USP, UVP, and other marketing messaging to ensure they're both compelling and authentic to your brand.

Your Path Forward

Positioning is the bridge between your vision and the clients you're meant to serve. By defining your ideal client, narrowing your niche, conducting thoughtful market research, and crafting a strong USP, you're laying the groundwork for a business that stands out and attracts the right people.

With your positioning solidified, you're ready to move to the next phase: **Packaging**. Here, you'll design irresistible offers that align with your audience's needs and your business goals.

4

Form Your Offer: Packaging Solutions that Sell

The Art of Packaging Your Offer

Your offer is the heart of your business. It's how you deliver value, solve problems, and create transformation for your clients. Packaging isn't just about deciding what you'll sell; it's about designing a solution that aligns with your goals, reflects your expertise, and resonates with the people you're meant to serve.

In this chapter, you'll learn how to create a core offer that meets your audience's needs, set pricing that reflects your value, and build a value ladder that supports long-term business growth. This is where your vision becomes tangible, and your business begins to take shape.

Creating a Core Offer

Designing a Solution That Transforms

Your core offer is the primary way you deliver value to your clients. It should address a specific problem, offer a clear transformation, and align with your expertise. When designing your core offer, focus on simplicity and impact.

Exercise: Ask yourself:

- What is the primary problem my ideal client faces?
- What outcome do I want my offer to create for them?
- How does this solution reflect my unique skills and perspective?

Your offer should deliver a transformation that your clients can visualize and aspire to. Whether it's helping them achieve financial freedom, overcome a challenge, or create a life they love, your offer is the bridge between their current struggles and their desired success.

Example: If your ideal client struggles with launching a business, your core offer could be a coaching program that guides them step by step from idea to launch, providing clarity and confidence along the way.

Aligning Your Offer with Your Goals

Your business goals should guide the design of your core offer.

Exercise: Consider the following:

- How much revenue do I want to generate each month?
- How many clients can I realistically serve at once?

- What type of delivery model (1:1 coaching, group programs, digital products) aligns with my lifestyle?

By aligning your offer with your goals, you ensure it supports both your financial objectives and your desired lifestyle.

Setting a Pricing Strategy

Pricing for Value and Profitability

Pricing is one of the most challenging aspects of packaging, but it's also one of the most important. The right pricing reflects the value of your offer, positions you in the market, and ensures profitability.

Exercise: When setting your prices, consider:

- The transformation you're providing: What is the value of the outcome your client will achieve?
- Your desired income: How much do you need to charge to meet your financial goals?
- Market research: What are others charging for similar services, and how does your offer stand out?

Avoid underpricing out of fear or comparison. Remember, your pricing communicates the value and confidence you have in your offer.

Overcoming Pricing Fears

Many entrepreneurs struggle with charging what their services are worth, fearing they'll alienate potential clients. But here's the truth: the right clients will value the transformation you provide and will gladly invest in it. Pricing too low can undermine your credibility and make it harder to achieve your goals.

You are not just selling a service; you are offering a solution that changes lives. Don't be afraid to stand firm in the value you bring.

Building a Value Ladder

Offering Multiple Solutions

A value ladder (or offer suite) allows you to serve your clients at different stages of their journey, offering solutions that meet them where they are and guiding them toward higher-value offers as their needs evolve. This strategy not only increases revenue but also deepens client relationships over time.

Your value ladder might include:

1. **Entry-Level Offers**: Low-cost, high-value products or services that introduce clients to your work (e.g., workshops, eBooks, or mini-courses).

2. **Core Offers**: The primary way you deliver transformation (e.g., coaching programs, consulting packages, or online courses).

3. **Premium Offers**: High-ticket services for clients who want a more in-depth or personalized experience (e.g., VIP days, retreats, or long-term coaching).

By designing a value ladder, you create opportunities to serve a broader audience while increasing the lifetime value of each client.

Scaling Your Offers

Once your value ladder is in place, you can focus on scaling your business by optimizing your offers and systems. This might include automating your entry-level products, refining your core offer based on client feedback, or expanding your premium services.

Every step of your value ladder is an opportunity to make an impact. With each offer, you're not just growing your business; you're changing lives.

How Ready to Launch Simplifies This Process

Designing your core offer, pricing it effectively, and building a value ladder can feel overwhelming; but you don't have to figure it out alone. Inside the ***Ready to Launch Incubator***, we provide tools, templates, and expert guidance to simplify every step of the packaging process. From crafting a compelling offer to setting prices with confidence, we ensure you have everything you need to succeed.

Your Path Forward

Packaging is where your vision takes shape. By creating a core offer that transforms lives, pricing it to reflect its value, and building a value ladder to serve clients at every stage, you're laying the foundation for a profitable and sustainable business.

Next, we'll dive into the **Planning** phase. This is where you'll develop the marketing and sales strategies that bring your offers to life and connect you with the clients you're meant to serve.

5

Formulate Your Plan: Mapping Your Marketing and Sales Strategy

The Power of a Strategic Plan

You have a powerful vision, a clear offer, and the confidence to step into your role as a CEO. Now it's time to turn that vision into action. Planning is the bridge between dreaming and doing; it's where strategies are crafted, systems are built, and success begins to take shape.

This chapter focuses on creating a marketing and sales plan that connects your offer to the clients who need it most. You'll learn how to design strategies that align with your strengths, streamline your efforts, and set you up for sustainable growth.

Developing Your Marketing Strategy

Aligning Your Marketing with Your Strengths

Marketing is often seen as overwhelming, but it doesn't have to be. The key is to focus on strategies that align with your strengths *and* resonate with your audience. When you lean into what feels natural and authentic, marketing becomes less about selling and more about serving.

Exercise: Ask yourself:

- What platforms do I enjoy using, and where is my audience active?
- How do I best communicate—through writing, speaking, or visuals?
- What type of content resonates most with my ideal client?

Marketing isn't about shouting into the void. It's about building relationships. You already have the tools to connect; now it's about using them intentionally.

Building Awareness and Trust

The goal of marketing is to create awareness of your brand and build trust with your audience. This involves showing up consistently, sharing valuable information, and positioning yourself as the solution to your clients' challenges.

Focus on these pillars:

1. **Consistency**: Develop a schedule for posting, emailing, or engaging with your audience.

2. **Value**: Share content that educates, inspires, or solves a problem.

3. **Authenticity**: Be yourself. Your voice and perspective are your greatest assets.

Inside the ***Ready to Launch Incubator***, we provide a **Content Marketing Planner** to help you map out posts, emails, and campaigns that connect with your audience and drive engagement.

Creating a Content Plan

Crafting Content That Converts

Content is how you communicate your expertise, build trust, and guide your audience toward your offer. It's not just about posting; it's about creating intentional content that moves your audience from awareness to action.

Consider these types of content:

- **Educational Content**: Share tips, tutorials, or insights that showcase your expertise.
- **Storytelling Content**: Share your journey, client success stories, or behind-the-scenes moments to build connection.
- **Promotional Content**: Clearly explain your offer, its benefits, and how it transforms your clients' lives.

Tip: Use the "3:1 Rule": for every piece of promotional content, share three pieces of value-driven or relationship-building content.

Streamlining Your Content Creation

Consistency doesn't mean constant effort. By batching your content or using tools to automate scheduling, you can show up regularly without feeling overwhelmed.

Designing Your Sales Systems

Simplifying the Sales Process

Sales can feel intimidating, but with the right systems, it becomes a natural extension of your marketing efforts. Your sales process should guide potential clients through a journey that feels clear, supportive, and empowering.

Key elements of a strong sales system:

1. **Lead Capture**: Use opt-ins, freebies, or events to collect contact information from interested prospects.
2. **Nurturing**: Build relationships through follow-up emails, personalized outreach with valuable content.
3. **Conversion**: Create clear calls-to-action that guide prospects toward scheduling a call, purchasing, or signing up.

Selling isn't about convincing; it's about offering a solution. When you believe in your offer, sales becomes an act of service.

Automating for Efficiency

Automation allows you to focus on your zone of genius while your systems handle repetitive tasks. Tools like email marketing platforms, CRM systems, and scheduling apps can simplify your workflow and ensure no leads fall through the cracks.

Tip: Start small by automating one part of your sales process, such as sending welcome emails to new subscribers. Gradually build out your systems as your business grows.

How Ready to Launch Simplifies Planning

Planning doesn't have to feel overwhelming. In the ***Ready to Launch Incubator***, we provide step-by-step guidance and tools to simplify the planning process, including:

- A **Platform Evaluation Tool** designed to help you determine the best platforms to connect with your audience.
- A **Content Maketing Planner** to map out your posts and campaigns.
- A **Lead Magnet Planner** to help you design high-value lead magnets to grab your ideal client's attention.
- And, more!

With these resources, you can approach planning with confidence and clarity, knowing you have the support you need to succeed.

Your Path Forward

Planning is where your vision becomes actionable. By developing a thoughtful marketing strategy, crafting intentional content, and building streamlined sales systems, you're setting your business up for success. These plans are not just items on a checklist. They are the foundation of your connection with the clients you're meant to serve.

In the next chapter, we'll dive into **Promotion**, where you'll learn how to launch your business with confidence and attract the clients who are ready for your transformation.

6

Fuel Your Launch: Promote with Confidence and Simplicity

The Power of a Purposeful Launch

Your business is ready, your offers are solidified, and your systems are in place. Now, it's time to step boldly into the spotlight and share your work with the world. Promotion is about more than marketing; it's about creating excitement, building connections, and inviting your audience into the transformation you've designed for them.

A successful launch doesn't require perfection or endless complexity. It requires clarity, confidence, and a focus on systems that simplify your efforts. This chapter will guide you through creating a purposeful launch strategy and establishing systems that keep you focused on what matters most; serving your clients and growing your business.

Designing Your Launch Strategy

Setting Intentional Goals

A launch isn't just about making sales; it's about creating momentum for your business. Before you start, define clear goals that align with your vision. These might include revenue targets, audience growth, or building brand awareness.

Exercise: Ask yourself:

- What do I want to achieve with this launch?
- How will I measure success beyond financial results?
- How can I ensure my goals reflect both impact and income?

Every launch is a learning opportunity. Celebrate progress, not just outcomes, and trust that each step brings you closer to your larger vision.

Mapping Out Your Launch Timeline

A successful launch requires thoughtful planning and execution. Break your launch into three phases:

1. **Pre-Launch**: Build anticipation by engaging your audience with valuable content, sneak peeks, or exclusive opportunities.
2. **Launch**: Announce your offer, share the transformation it provides, and create urgency with limited-time bonuses or enrollment windows.
3. **Post-Launch**: Review your results, gather feedback, and nurture relationships with your new clients.

Tip: Keep your timeline realistic and flexible. Avoid overloading yourself, and focus on executing each phase with intention and clarity.

Simplifying Promotion with Systems

Automating Key Processes

Promotion can feel overwhelming, but systems and automation tools can simplify your efforts. From scheduling social media posts to automating email sequences, these tools allow you to focus on connecting with your audience instead of getting buried in repetitive tasks.

Consider automating:

- **Email Campaigns**: Create sequences that nurture leads and guide them toward your offer.
- **Content Scheduling**: Plan and schedule posts to keep your audience engaged throughout the launch and beyond.
- **Lead Management**: Use CRM tools to track interactions and ensure no potential client falls through the cracks.

The *Ready to Launch Incubator* provides a comprehensive Asset Creation Planner and Launch Planner to help you streamline and build a repeatable and stress-free launch process.

Staying Organized with Checklists and Templates

A launch involves many moving parts, but staying organized can make the process manageable. Use checklists to track tasks and templates to streamline your communications... all of which are included in ***Ready to Launch***.

Engaging Your Audience

Building Excitement and Connection

Promotion is about creating energy around your offer. Engage your audience by sharing your story, highlighting the transformation your offer provides, and inviting them to take the next step.

Ways to build excitement:

- Host a live Q&A or webinar to answer questions and demonstrate your expertise.
- Share client testimonials or case studies that illustrate your offer's impact.
- Use countdowns or limited-time bonuses to create urgency.

Your audience is waiting for the solution you provide. Show up authentically, and trust that the right clients will respond to your message.

Gathering Feedback

Your launch is an opportunity to learn about your audience and refine your approach. Ask for feedback from participants to understand what resonated and what could be improved.

Tip: Send a post-launch survey to your email list or host a follow-up conversation with clients. Use the information they share to improve future launches and better serve your audience.

How Ready to Launch Supports Your Promotion

Launching doesn't have to feel overwhelming. Inside the *Ready to Launch Incubator*, you'll find step-by-step guidance to create a launch strategy that works for you. From timeline templates to automation tools, we provide everything you need to simplify your promotion and focus on what you do best; serving your clients and building a business you love.

Your Path Forward

Promotion is where preparation meets action. By designing an aligned launch strategy and simplifying your efforts with systems, you're setting yourself up for a successful start and sustainable growth. Remember, every launch is a chance to refine, grow, and connect with the people you're meant to serve.

In the next phase of your journey, continue building on the momentum you've created. Celebrate your progress, trust the process, and know that you're creating a business that reflects your purpose, values, and brilliance.

7

Finish Strong: Commit, Execute, and Step Fully Into Your CEO Role

Recapping the Ready to Launch Framework

Congratulations! You've now walked through the transformative steps of the ***Ready to Launch Framework***:

1. **Preparation**: Building a strong foundation with clarity, alignment, and a CEO mindset.

2. **Positioning**: Defining your niche, identifying your ideal client, and creating your market advantage.

3. **Packaging**: Crafting irresistible offers, setting pricing strategies, and building a value ladder/offer suite.

4. **Planning**: Developing marketing strategies, content plans, and sales systems.

5. Promotion: Launching your business with confidence and simplicity.

Each step has brought you closer to building a business that aligns with your purpose, serves your audience, and creates the life you've envisioned. But this is just the beginning.

Following a Framework and Committing to the Work

Success doesn't come from winging it; it comes from committing to a proven process. The *Ready to Launch Framework* provides the structure, clarity, and guidance you need to move from an idea to a profitable, purpose-driven business. By following this framework and putting in consistent effort, you'll be equipped to overcome challenges, avoid overwhelm, and create meaningful impact.

You already have what it takes to succeed. The framework is your roadmap; your commitment is the fuel that will carry you forward. Stay focused, trust the process, and believe in your ability to create something extraordinary.

Leveraging Your Professional Expertise in Entrepreneurship

One of the greatest misconceptions about starting a business is the belief that you need to start from scratch. But the truth is, the skills, knowledge, and expertise you've developed throughout your career are invaluable assets in entrepreneurship. From problem-solving and communication to leadership and project management, these abilities transfer seamlessly into building and running a successful business.

Exercise: Think about the professional wins you've achieved. What skills made those successes possible? How can you apply those same abilities to your entrepreneurial journey? The experiences you bring to the table are your unique edge, so lean into them.

All You Need is an Idea and a Strategic Process

At its core, entrepreneurship is about solving problems. If you have an idea that provides a solution people are willing to pay for, you already have the foundation of a business. The key is taking that idea and following a strategic process to bring it to market.

The *Ready to Launch Framework* is that process. It guides you from refining your idea to launching your business with clarity and confidence. You don't need to reinvent the wheel or figure it out alone; the roadmap is here for you. Your responsibility is to take the first step and commit to the journey.

You don't need to have everything figured out. Start with your idea, follow the process, and trust that each step will build upon the last. Progress, not perfection, is the path to success.

Your Next Step

You're ready to move from dreaming to doing. Here's how you can take action today:

Book a Next Best Steps Strategy Call: Let's discuss your business idea, goals, and the type of support you need to achieve those goals.

TheAlignedBizCo.com/nbs-call

If you are ready to take the next step and know that the Ready to Launch Framework is the plan and process you need to launch your business with simplicity, ease, and alignment, enroll now at

AlignAndProsperAcademy.com/enroll-rtl

You have everything you need to succeed: the vision, the skills, and the framework. Now it's time to take action. Trust yourself, embrace the process, and remember, every step you take brings you closer to the life and business you desire and deserve.

This is your moment to rise, align, and prosper.